Long Ago AND Far Away

MESOPOTAMIA

Tamra Orr

PURPLE TOAD
PUBLISHING

PURPLE TOAD
PUBLISHING

Printing
1   2   3   4   5   6   7   8   9

Long Ago
AND
Far Away

Ancient China
Ancient Egypt
Ancient Rome
The Aztecs
Mesopotamia

Publisher's Cataloging-in-Publication Data
Orr, Tamra.
  Mesopotamia / Tamra Orr.
    p. cm.
Includes bibliographic references and index.
ISBN 9781624691300
1. Iraq—Civilization—To 634—Juvenile literature. I. Series: Long ago and far away.
 DS69 2015
 935
                                    Library of Congress Control Number: 2014945184

eBook ISBN: 9781624691317

ABOUT THE AUTHOR

Tamra Orr is the author of more than 350 nonfiction books for readers of all ages. She has written a number of books about ancient cultures and countries. She is a graduate of Ball State University in Muncie, Indiana, and moved to the Pacific Northwest in 2001. She is mom to four and an avid reader, letter writer, and music lover. For Orr, the best thing about being an author is learning all about the world, past and present, and sharing it with the rest of her family.

PUBLISHER'S NOTE

This book has been researched in depth, and to the best of our knowledge is correct. Although every measure is taken to give an accurate account, Purple Toad Publishing makes no warranty of the accuracy of the information and is not liable for damages caused by inaccuracies.

Contents

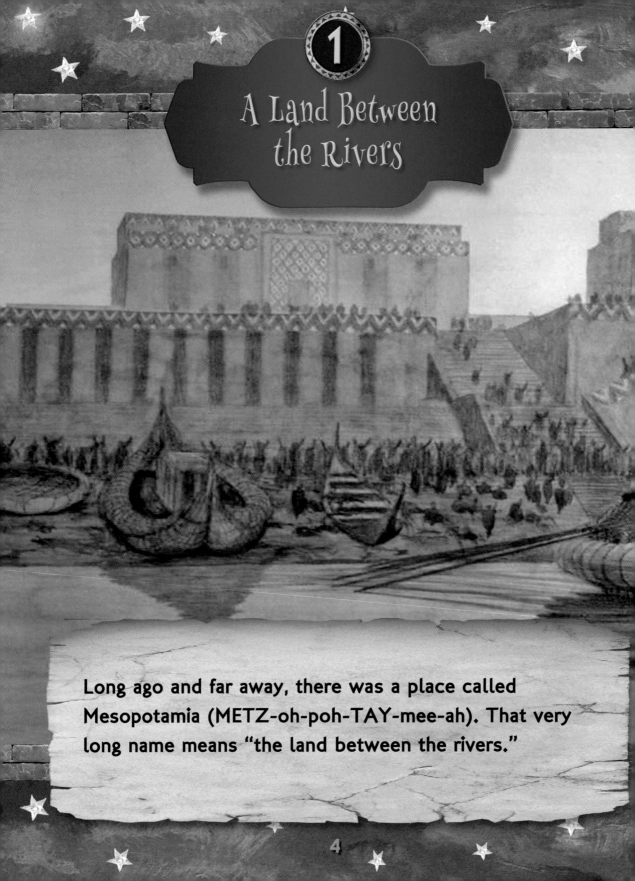

1

A Land Between the Rivers

Long ago and far away, there was a place called Mesopotamia (METZ-oh-poh-TAY-mee-ah). That very long name means "the land between the rivers."

North
America

Eur

A

Mesopotamia was in the Middle East. When you look at a world map, can you find Iraq? That is where Mesopotamia used to be. If you look closely, you can see that the land is between two long rivers. One is the Tigris (TY-gris). One is the Euphrates (yoo-FRAY-teez). Each of these rivers is more than one thousand miles long. The river water helped make the soil healthy for growing crops. Many groups of people settled there to farm the land.

Asia
IRAQ
Middle East
TURKEY
ARMENIA
Yerevan
AZERBAIJAN
Baku
Erzurum
Adana
Türkmenbashi
CYPRUS
Nicosia
Aleppo
Tabrīz
Mediterranean Sea
Beirut
LEBANON
SYRIA
Mosul
ISRAEL
Damascus
Tel Aviv-Yafo
Jerusalem
Amman
De Facto Boundary
Tigris
Euphrates
Tehrān
Suez Canal
Baghdad
JORDAN
Armistice Line
IRAQ
IRAN
Elat
EGYPT
Eşfahān
Tabūk
Al Başrah
Ābādān
Nile
Kuwait
KUWAIT
Shīrāz
Bandar-e Būshehr
Aswān
SAUDI ARABIA
Persian Gulf
Red
Bandar-e 'Abbās
Dhahran
Manama
BAHRAIN
QATAR
Riyadh
Doha
Abu Dhabi

Around 5000 BCE, that's 7000 years ago, these settlements grew into cities. They lasted for thousands of years. The people were very smart. They had great ideas that are still helpful today. Some of their inventions were so important that Mesopotamia had another name: "the cradle of civilization."

The Mesopotamian city of Ur

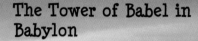

The Tower of Babel in
Babylon

Into the City-States

What was it like to live in this land so long ago?
Mesopotamia was not one large country. Instead, it was
made up of many city-states. These were like very big
cities. Each one was a little different from the next. Some
of the cities had 50,000 people. Some had more than
twice that! The biggest city was Babylon (BAB-uh-lon). It
had more than 200,000 people in it. Other cities were
Uruk, Akkad, Nimrud, and Persepolis (per-SEH-poh-lis).

The people in the different city-states did not always get along. In fact, they fought a lot! Empires grew and fell. They battled over land and water. They built tall walls around their cities to keep others out. Armies of soldiers rode in chariots from one place to the next. Chariots were like today's scooters. They held only one or two people. They were pulled by animals instead of engines.

The entrance to city-state Persepolis was called the Gate of Nations, and it is now being restored to its full glory.

A Mesopotamian chariot

2

Of Gods and Kings

The people of Mesopotamia believed in many gods. They prayed to them for good crops. They prayed to get better when they were sick. They prayed for more rain or less heat.

Religious symbols could be found all around the city-states. Artists made statues of the gods, and people put clothes on them. They brought them food. They washed them every day. They felt this was a way to honor the gods and keep them happy.

A sculputre of the goddess Ishtar, and statues of worshippers

Another way to show the gods respect was by building temples. People could go to a temple to honor a god. One type of temple is a ziggurat. If you wanted to climb to the top of one, you would need to take a few deep breaths. It would be a long trip. The ziggurat was usually built in the middle of the city-state. It had many levels, and each one was a little smaller than the one below it. On the outside were sets of stairs. The top of the ziggurat was flat.

Many buildings surrounded the temples. Schools met in some of these buildings; priests lived in others. The king also lived in buildings close to the ziggurat.

A Ruler from the Gods

The people of Mesopotamia were ruled by kings. They believed these kings were related to the gods and had great power. Kings lived in fancy palaces with many rooms. In fact, some of the palaces had the first flush toilets in history. They even had marble seats.They told the armies when to fight and where. They also had servants. Many people worked for the rulers, including judges, priests, and scribes.

Examples of
ziggurats

3

A, B, C and 1, 2, 3

If it were not for the people of Mesopotamia, you might not be able to read at all. Why? They invented one of the earliest forms of writing.

The only people who were taught how to write were men called scribes. They started going to school at the age of six, and they stayed until they were grown up. They used a stylus as a pen. It was made out of a long plant called a reed. Scribes used soft clay instead of paper. They used the stylus to press shapes into the clay, then left the clay out to harden. Some of the shapes were lines. Some were circles. Some were half moons or dots. Over time, more shapes were added.

Scribes wrote letters for the kings. They wrote down very long stories and poems. These often told about the adventures of gods, kings, and other heroes. Because of their skill, scribes were some of the most important people in the city-state.

Scribes and
their writings

Number Time

Scribes also used numbers. They were the first to find a way of counting. They kept track of taxes. They wrote down how many sheep one farmer had, or how much wheat another one grew. They based their counting system on the number 60. Can you think of things that are still divided into 60 units? How many seconds are in a minute? How many minutes in an hour? You guessed it: 60!

Scribes also measured things and wrote them down. What did they use to measure things? A tiny piece of corn! Some Mesopotamians watched the skies very carefully, too. They learned all about how the stars, sun, and moon moved. They wrote it all down. They were some of the first people to do that!

Along with kings, priests, judges, and scribes, craftspeople and merchants lived in Mesopotamia. These people bought, sold, and traded cloth, tools, art, pottery, and food.

Some of the people living in Mesopotamia were servants. They spent their lives working for the king and his people. Some were working off a debt, or money they owed. Other slaves were people who had been captured in battle. Slaves did not have any rights and were not protected by any laws. They were usually treated kindly, however.

Slaves even had to build whole cities.

4

Life on the Farm

Not everyone lived in palaces and fancy homes like kings, priests, judges, and scribes. Merchants, artists, and slaves lived on farms outside the city-state in small, square houses. A few of the tools they invented changed how farming was done. Some, such as a simple plow, are still being used today.

Farmers in Mesopotamia grew wheat and barley. They grew fruit trees and vegetables. They knew that crops needed water. Since they lived between two rivers, water was close, but they had to invent a way to get it to their crops. The farmers dug canals. These allowed the water to run from rivers and springs into the fields. Farmers also set up barrels to collect rain when it fell.

Inventing Tools

Have you ever seen a plow out in a field? Plows were invented by the Mesopotamians! Seeder plows had long tubes. The seed would drop down the tube. Then it would fall into the soil as the farmer plowed the earth. Mesopotamian farmers also built carts. They started with pieces of wood. They added sides. Then they invented the wheel! They added the wheels to the cart. They were the first people to do this!

    To carry their foods and other goods up or down the river, the people also built boats. They made rafts out of logs and animal skins. They were the first people to add sails to their boats and make use of the wind.

Plows helped farmers then and now.

5

Come In the House

If you were going to build a house, what would you use? What if you lived where there were very few trees for wood? What if there were no stones or rocks? This was the problem for the people in Mesopotamia. What could they use? There were two things they had a lot of: muddy clay from the rivers, and reeds, a type of strong, grassy plant.

The Mesopotamians bundled bunches of reeds together. They packed and tied them together very tightly, and they used these bundles to make simple homes. Reeds were used to make the roof and doors too.

Stronger houses were made when people took muddy clay from the river and mixed it with straw. They shaped this mixture into large blocks, and then let the blocks dry in the hot sun. These sturdy blocks were used to build the walls of houses.

A house made
from reeds.

Houses rarely had windows, as there was no glass yet. Roofs were sometimes flat. Why? In the hot summer months, the family could crawl out on the roof to sleep. It was much cooler there—and who doesn't like to sleep under the stars?

Inside most houses, there was very little furniture. While wooden chairs, tables, and beds were found in kings' palaces, most homes used simple mats and rugs made of reeds woven together. Some homes had benches built into their walls. What were they made of? Clay and mud, of course!

The people in Mesopotamia lived a very long time ago. Life was quite different then. Boys and girls still liked to play, though. They went swimming. They played with jump ropes and spinning tops. They tossed balls through hoops. They played with dolls and toys made out of clay. They had fun all those years ago, just as you do today!

Ancient clay
pull toy

Further Reading

Books

Apte, Sunita. *Mesopotamia*. Danbury, CT: True Books, 2010.

Doeden, Matt. *Tools and Treasures of Ancient Mesopotamia*. Minneapolis, MN: Lerner Publications, 2014.

Feinstein, Stephen. *Discover Ancient Mesopotamia*. Berkeley Heights, NJ: Enslow Publishers, 2014.

Morley, Jacqueline. *You Wouldn't Want to be a Sumerian Slave! A Life of Hard Labor You'd Rather Avoid*. New York: Franklin Watts, 2007.

Samuels, Charlie. *Technology in Mesopotamia*. New York: Gareth Stevens, 2013.

Works Consulted

Bertman, Stephen. *Handbook of Life in Ancient Mesopotamia*. Facts on File, New York, 2003

Kriwaczek, Paul. *Babylon: Mesopotamia and the Birth of Civilization*. St. Martin's Griffin, 2012.

Nissen, Hans. *From Mesopotamia to Iraq: A Concise History*. University of Chicago Press, 2009.

On the Internet

"Ancient Civilizations for Kids: Ancient Iraq (Mesopotamia)"
https://sites.google.com/site/1ancientcivilizationsforkids/ancient-iraq-mesopotamia

"Ancient Mesopotamia/Great Cities of Mesopotamia" Duckster.com.
http://www.ducksters.com/history/mesopotamia/great_cities_of_ancient_mesopotamia.php

Millburn, Naomi. "The Use of the Sail in Ancient Mespotamia." Demand Media, Undated.
http://classroom.synonym.com/use-sail-ancient-mesopotamia-10077.html

Glossary

barley—a type of grain

canal—a man-made waterway

chariot—an ancient two-wheeled horse-drawn vehicle

city-states—a large city that could govern itself

cradle of civilization— a location identified as the site where a civilization began

debt—an amount of money owed to someone

merchant—someone who buys and sells goods or products

pottery—dishes and jars made with baked clay

priest—a minister or religious leader

reed—a tall water plant

scribe—a person trained in writing and recording documents

soil—dirt

stylus—a pen or writing instrument

temple—a religious building for worshiping a god

ziggurat—an ancient temple

Index